WHERE THE TIME WENT:
POEMS AT EIGHTY

December 2018

- For Joan and Warren —
with very best wishes
and sincere thanks for
your support —
My hope is that you
will enjoy the words on
these pages —
Clem Schoenebeck

WHERE THE TIME WENT:
POEMS AT EIGHTY

CLEMENS CARL SCHOENEBECK

Encircle Publications, LLC
Farmington, Maine USA

Where the Time Went: Poems at Eighty Copyright ©2018 Clemens Carl Schoenebeck

ISBN-13: 978-1-948338-23-3

Editor: Cynthia Brackett-Vincent

Book and book cover design: Eddie Vincent/ENC Graphics Services
Cover Illustration: Angela Baldacci
Author photograph: Yoon S. Byun

Printing: Walch Publishing, Portland, Maine

Mail Orders, Author Inquiries:
Encircle Publications
PO Box 187
Farmington, ME 04938
207-778-0467

Online orders:
http://encirclepub.com

PUBLICATION ACKNOWLEDGEMENTS

The following poetry journals and magazines have published poems in this collection, some in slightly different forms:

Adept Press—"Broom-clean"; "Drumbeat"; "First Day of School"; "Tea Party"
The Aurorean—"A Different Breathing"; "A Little Night Music"; "Angela's Mantra"; "Aunt Mary's Table"; "Praying at 10,000 feet"; "Classic Shoe Shine, $3.00"; "Collected Coins"; "December Gift"; "Dreamcatcher"; "For the Angels, Unwinged"; "Howell's Mandolin"; "Kristen"; "On the Death of T-Shirts"; "Prayer in my pocket"; "Saturday Morning at the Tilton Diner"; "Shoe Shine"; "Simple Wood"; "Venus and the Waxing Moon"
Caribbean Writer—"Anguilla Cemetery"
Dan River Anthology—"Alto, in the Second Row"; "Crested Butte Sunrise"; "How He Listens"; "Perseids"; "Sixty Candles"; "Snowplow Man"
Miramar Poetry Journal—"After Haydn"; "Old Dog"
Northwoods Anthology—"Inheritance"; "Recess at Machon Elementary"
Parkinson's Magazine—"Parkinson's"
Reader's Break—"Lamentation"; "November Gray"
Tufts Dental Magazine—"Baggage Claim."
Writer's World—"Full Sail."

These poems have placed in the following contests or venues:

"Crescendo, by Ozawa and the B.S.O."—Poetry for Rockport (2nd prize, Massachusetts State Poetry National Contest)
"Full Sail"—Marblehead Festival of Arts (Best of Show; Marcia Doehner Award)
"Resurrection"— Naomi Cherkofsky Contest (2nd place)
"Sunset, Late November"— Amy Dengler Contest (3rd place)
"Tea Party"—(3rd prize, Massachusetts State Poetry National Contest).

The following poems have also been nominated for the Pushcart Prize: "For the Angels, Unwinged"; "Kristen"; "Broom-clean."

DEDICATION

for my teachers

Sophie, Bonnie, Kristen, Alexa, Angela

CONTENTS

have patience with everything unresolved in your heart
and to try to love the *questions themselves*
as if they were locked rooms or books written
in a very foreign language.
Don't search for the answers,
which could not be given to you now,
because you would not be able to live them.
And the point is, to live everything.
Live the questions now.

~ Rainer Maria Rilke ~
(*Letters to a Young Poet*, translated by Stephen Mitchell)

HOW POETRY FOUND ME

It did not stalk or pursue me, nor was I hiding from it. Poetry came to me when I was most vulnerable. Moments after her birth, I saw my first grandchild cradled in my daughter's arms. Swaddled in a white wrap, pink cap on her head, Alexa was staring into her mother's eyes with such intensity that nothing would come between them. These words came to me, mysterious, resonant and clear: *They have been here forever.*

Bonnie and I drove home on that chill December night. Christmas lights glowed bright and white around the perimeter of Salem Common. The stars shimmered with such clarity that I felt I could reach up and pick them right out of the dark night. I could easily read the obediently arranged constellations. For that moment, the North Star was mine.

I did the only thing I could do. I went home and picked up my pen.

I wrote a letter of welcome for my granddaughter, a Christmas present for her mother. Throbbing with good will and newly inspired love, my words blurred the page with emotion. But I'd penned enough meaningful imagery and truth that my wife and daughter said to me, "Pay attention."

I paid attention. I read Mary Oliver's *Rules for the Dance.* I attended lectures and signed up for Jeanette Maes' workshops. I was captivated by Bill Moyers' popular TV series, *The Language of Life.* I learned that poetry did not have to be garbed in academic robes and recited from a lofty ivory tower. It could be a shared conversation made meaningful by carefully arranged words, moving forward by the momentum of its own rhythm. My friend Dennis Must, an award-winning writer, mentored me in my early writing. He encouraged me to share my words.

My earliest poems were submitted to *the Aurorean.* The publisher has always been supportive of new writers. I will never forget the thrill of seeing my own work between the covers of a respected poetry journal. Cynthia Brackett-Vincent's encouragement lit up the path to my own creativity.

Now I do the only thing I can do. I keep my pen full and look for the next poem.

MUSIC & FLIGHT

A DIFFERENT BREATHING

Christmas in Boston; Handel-Haydn Choir, *Messiah*.
The bold tenor demands certain priorities:
Every valley shall be exalted,
Every mountain made low,
The crooked made straight,
   The rough places, plain.

As if I don't get the message, he thrills
the valley line, trembles the word *exalted*, lifting
the syllable *al* with flowing melismatic steps, stretching
to a lush legato *aaall*, as in the word, *all*; as in
that includes you, buddy, slouched in seat 2, row C, balcony B,
where he finds me in *my* wilderness, aims the prayer at me,
  punctuating and offering that redeeming word, *Exalted!*

May I tell you,
    I was filled; I'd inhaled the prayer.
    What I carried nurtured me.
May I tell you,
    I held my breath protectively, like a shepherd guarding
    his flock of sheep, as I went out into that December shiver.
I must tell you,
    when I exhaled, my breath went out from me
    in ways I do not understand; a white ghost, it preceded me,
and I followed, as if it were whispering *prepare ye the way...*
I must tell you,
    it was inhaled by someone cold, in a dark alley,
by someone in an apartment with one dim light,
by someone who needed my warm and holy air more than I did.
I am forced to tell you; there is no other way to say this...
    They were the better for it.
    And so was I.

ALTO, IN THE SECOND ROW

for Bonnie

Because she can't read music,
she stands behind those who can.

Just shy of the higher octave,
her notes tiptoe up and down the scale
seeking buoyancy in the stream of voices.

At Thursday evening's rehearsal,
she traps the choir in her CTR-122 recorder
from Radio Shack, with its sensitive ears.

Once home, the music is released,
organ, director, laughter and all.
Amazing Grace lifts like a rainbow
over the cloudburst of her shower.
Emphatic *hallelujahs* sweep clean
through the Hoover's strained monotone.

Sunday worship comes.
The chorus sings
and she brings wings beneath
the soprano's soaring song.

Her *Heart is in a Holy Place...*

BRAHMS IN SUMMER

It seems *ein Deutsches Requiem*
should be sung In November, accompanied
by its austere unfolding of diminishment,
fading light and ebbing warmth, singers
cloaked darkly in best dresses and suits,
somber neckties and polished black shoes.

But it's July and my daylilies are exploding
like fireworks on the Fourth, and even Brahms
recognizes our impermanence: *the glory of man
flowers before it withereth and falleth away.*

So we are dressed in T-shirts and shorts,
gauzy blouses and slacks, and I can't believe
how good we're all singing in our pickup chorus
lifted by the energy of our conductor who wants
that vowel right on the downbeat, keeping time
with Johannes' prescribed pace (don't slow down)

because we can't wait for the solemnity of winter.
It's not too early to look up at the bouquet exploded
in the holiday night, its graceful arc of spent roses
and daisies patient in their own withering and falling.

Not too early to look into the timeless and forever night,
punctuated by its celestial assembly of constellations
and hopeful stars, and sing softly at moderate tempo,
wie lieblich sind deine Wohnungen and contemplate
How lovely is thy dwelling place, O Lord of Hosts!
Not too early—or too late—to comfort those that mourn.

There is time, still time to bloom.

A DAY FOR PALESTRINA

Giovanni P. da Palestrina
Composer (1525-1594)

From the organ,
Nami sounds the pitch.
Outside the open window,
trees stand tall in green attention,
subdue their leafy flutter.

Sicut Cervus the brave tenors lead.
Dependable altos, sparkling sopranos,
determined basses echo their entrances.
We are lifted, *de si de rat ad fontes aquarum*

as each of us weaves our strand of harmony
into the tapestry, until we detach from gravity,
anima mea ad te Deus; then our descent
to our semi-circle on earth, the sun-filled earth.

Behind his closed eyes,
we were Reverend Vann's meditation.
We'd blurred Tom Lunt's eye and
carried Linda Lee to a great cathedral,
our notes swirling in the high vault.

And were we that good?
We searched our conductor's eyes,
already on us, wide, a hint of surprise;
then Francie touched her lips, extended
fingers, palm open and up and blew thanks.

Yes, we were that good.
The trees resumed swaying,
four beats to the measure, as they
shimmered in green applause and
our notes streamed out into the world,
above and through the sunny hopeful world,
without end, Amen, and our pastor said
                    sing it again.

A LITTLE NIGHT MUSIC

from Mozart's *Eine Kleine Nachtmusik*

In the transparent dark of a New Hampshire night,
stars and constellations brush the tops of trees,
shining big and white, like an unblemished soul.

My face tilts to the haze of The Milky Way,
the regal glare of Orion's sword, Perseid's Shooting Stars,
which dazzle and die, in the blink of an eye.

High in the hills I hear, *ow-ooh,* from the lead coyote,
a pause, then pure-pitched echoes sung
by the Alpha's answering chorus.

I turn to those singers, my head thrown back,
arms like a maestro leading a hymn.
Ow-ooh, I howl, glancing off *Owww,*
lifting nearly an octave to *Ooh...*

Somewhere between mountain and stars,
they answer *Ow-Ooh,* holding the *Oooohhh*
in a long thread of sound, a
layering of distant harmonies...

Above the stunning silence,
the celestial assembly stirs, then glows,
glitters and shimmers in Heavenly ovation...

CRESCENDO, BY OZAWA AND THE B.S.O.

As if tethered by unseen wires,
the musicians stroke their violins in time
with the Maestro's dancing hands,
like puppets and puppeteer.

Ozawa chops Beethoven
into staccato slices,
flings notes
of musical confetti.

His fingers float, then wilt
into a shrinking diminuendo,
which he caresses,
like a broken-winged bird
against his breast.

Rising on tiptoes,
he stretches an arpeggio,
hands climbing a ladder
of resonant chords.

His trembling arms bear-hug
the swelling sound until
it cannot be restrained.
He surrenders, unfolds
a roaring crescendo,
still stuck in my ear.

THURSDAY NIGHT REHEARSAL

for Frances Fitch

There are the usual reasons for choir practice:
New music and words, a sense of when to breathe.
Beyond that, the lofty goal of flight.
Perhaps, even to soar.

Francie is the apex of our flying constellation,
Boss Goose, who navigates her singers
through the turbulence of the unknown
until the unfamiliar becomes familiar
through the faith of repetition, and flapping wings.

Our director implores, cajoles, never scolds.
Diction is done with the tip of the tongue on the teeth.
Let's all sing the bass line, pickup at bar thirty-three.
Nami, give me a C.

The time comes, and it *almost* always comes,
when the layers of harmony coalesce
and we begin to glide, feel at home in the sky;
eagles, momentarily Pavarottied, possessed by Bach,

Francie, our sober pilot, eases
her intoxicated crew back to earth,
where once again, we have weight.
See you Sunday morning. Don't be late!

It is not what we hear,
or the sound we sing, but
more of a feeling, a giddiness, how
for a few moments each week,
we become untethered from gravity.

HOWELL'S MANDOLIN

He performs most summer days
sitting on a bench overlooking Red Rock,
embracing his mandolin, strumming double-strings.
The empty case rests, open and hopeful at his feet.

He plucks notes, throws them like delicate darts
into the surging tide, thrums major cords electric,
arcing to clouds; perhaps energy for future lightning?
The Atlantic thumps its rhythmic applause.

First time I saw him, I walked on by.
Next day I fluttered a dollar into the blue-lined case,
gifting it with a sparse touch of green. Later on
I shared his bench and learned his name.

Howell. Played Carnegie Hall. I was a child.
His eyes glisten as he remembers gifts he had.
A solo. Five years old. He soothes himself with
something in a paper bag, brought to his lips, then

tells me the mandolin was meant for classical and
Bach is best. He picks it up, transforms us both with
Jesu, Joy of Man's Desiring, as notes gather and soar,
rising like eagles kettling on an updraft. To the south,

buildings of Boston's skyline stand in rapt attention.
Right above us, a jetliner, Lufthansa, departing Logan,
ascends in its flight to Germany, its lift a miracle
of the physics of wind and wing and Bach.

HOW IT STAYS WITH ME

for Maria van Kalken

Festival Chorus, 2011
The concert is over, but the music doesn't stop,
said Max and both Andrews, to the newcomer.

Who knows what triggers it? A cell phone's ring, in middle C?
The baritone thrum of a passing car? The music won't rest.
A car door's percussive thump starts *Be-te-le-he-mu!*

In the parish hall of the memory center, where neurons
bind and gag the learned music, the choir awaits its cue
to release all hostages in remembered performance.

Lights flicker on and off. It's time. Women smooth wrinkles
from their long black dresses. Men tug and tighten red ties.
Sip of cold water, cough drop, quick trip to the head?

We process through the Church of Gray Matter, *Vom himmel hoch.*
Maria, tall on her stand, lifts her hands as if blessing the choir,
a hundred voices tethered in time, shaping the air between us.

I hear the wispy clink of wind chimes, and Mike is at the keyboard,
feathering those up and down Rutter riffs in Movement II, the
peaks and valleys like an EKG on the score. My heart beats in time.

That *Jubilato* line in Pinkham sticks in my mind: altos echo sopranos,
intertwined notes fluttering like angel wings, the metronomic joining
on *Dominum in lae-ti-ti-a* and I must remember my *Gloria* entrance.

Afterward, Gabrielli blasts from the car behind, startling me awake
to the light gone red to green. In the mirror, the driver scowls at me.
I rhythmically step on the gas, *that I from thee may quickly part.*

But only after lifting two rousing *Alleluias*, conducted
with a questionable gesture; one for me, and one
for the man who needs music in his heart.

AFTER HAYDN

for Alex and her father

I observe fathers with
their daughters, because
I'm father to a daughter.

I know her gentle tug
on my arm, the caressed guidance
around the ice patch I don't see.

It's an age thing now,
this rebalanced love, as
the daughter mothers the father.

After our choir rehearsed Haydn,
The Benedictus still resonant within us,
I watched my friend with his daughter,

remembered the angle of their leaning
against each other, arms intertwined
as they walked from Old North Church,

entering, then disappearing into the winter night…

THE SPACE BETWEEN

for Francie Fitch and Roy Correnti

We're three at the table.
Roy's on my left, Francie, my right.
I face the space between.

Sunday after Thanksgiving,
I lead our worship; Francie, the music.
We're planning our prayers and hymns.

Roy *is* the sermon.
A fisherman with a golden net,
he's trapped God within.

He'll soon trade walker for wheelchair,
as his space between muscles and nerves
clogs from the orange sludge of 'nam.

As his space between word and song,
his praying and singing and healing,
coughs with the orange breath of 'nam.

Francie leans to Roy, invites
his request for the choir.
His eyes smile a remembrance.

He woke up in the hospital,
fifteen years ago,
Judy Collins on the radio.

The transfusion of her song healed
the space between addiction and recovery.
Was blind, but now he sees...

Amazing Grace, Roy croaks, raspy and rough.
How sweet the sound, Francie answers.
Their duet begins,

That saved a wretch like me.
Her voice puts meat on his thin words.
I once was lost, but now I'm found.

Francie slows the tempo, burnishes the edge
of Roy's splintered sound, whispering through
verse two; *the hour I first believed.*

His heavy prayer, lifted by offered wings,
ends in a laborious soaring, his air expelled;
And grace will lead us home…

Silence…
The space between, filled
by the gift given and the gift received.

An incandescence,
more felt than seen;
A Truth, that cannot be uttered in this poem.

SHELTER MUSIC

for Andrew Oliver

The picture, sent days after the event, touches me as deeply
as the music itself. The photograph sweeps the concert hall,
dining room minus tables. It scans the watchful audience,
which for today lives under this roof, in predictable warmth.
The residents of Lifebridge listen deeply, some slightly bent

by what they carry; a durable weariness of nights in the cold.
I, who can touch a thermostat, cannot see what bends them,
but we lean together into this music, listening for possibilities.
I see myself in the middle of this crowd, guest of my friend
seated next to me. He believes *a man's home is his castle.*

On my other side, a woman with tired blond hair, her sad eyes
arguing against the light. I remember how the early measures
of Torelli throbbed me. This woman rocked *back and forth,*
back and forth, in time with the two violinists and the cellist.
I thought of my own mother swaying in her rocking chair,

back and forth, trying to escape her voices and I nearly wept.
The picture shows a man wearing a knit hat, another with big
muscles and a Patriots cap, a woman caressing whatever warmth
lingers in her Styrofoam coffee cup. They could be my family, a
brother or a cousin, related by how we are taken into the music,

this gift of three women playing with such generosity. Now there
is a break, time for a friendly chat by the first violinist. She asks
How many have played an instrument? Eight or nine hands go up.
Some laughter, then more music. It's Haydn and it just melts me.
I close my eyes and feel my mother swaying next to me.

DRUMBEAT

My time is here, my time is now.
Days whisper quickly by.
The hours brush upon my brow,
like trees against the sky.

The moment flows, it cannot wait.
Its rhythm drums too loud.
The minutes dance upon my fate,
like raindrops from a cloud.

The meter shows, it will impose
each breath's allotted air.
The cadence slows, it only slows,
when floating through a prayer...

EXODUS

I'm at my dining room table, meditating
on Handel's oratorio, *Israel in Egypt,*
marching music for their escape from slavery
as Moses leads the tribe to the Promised Land.

My coffee cup is warm in my hands
and I'm looking out my window, looking
across Nahant Bay, past Boston Harbor where
the slate-blue ribbon of the South Shore breaks

the winter-cold ocean from the rose blush of sunrise.
I consider four friends chained to their own darkness:
tremors, cancer, divorce, and a muddled mind.
My coffee is cooling, and the sunrise as well.

Then flickers a beacon, incandescent red,
reflected off a window fifteen miles distant,
near Nantasket or Cohasset or some source
unmapped and unknowable as it flares and flames.

Soon the light is extinguished; the sun has stolen fire
from the burning bush. My cup is empty, and I can only pray
for a lit path for my friends, deliverance from their wilderness,
to a place of milk and honey.

BELL RINGER

for Jane Kraybill

Types of bells:
Altar bell, Handbell, Carillon and Chime,
Cowbell, Jingle bell, Glockenspiel, Babendil.
Sail away on a Ship Bell's clang.

Sounding Patterns of Bells:
Change ringing, Random ringing,
Full Circle and Small Arc Swinging;
the physics of pendulum swaying
and playing, *ding dong* the bell's song.

Notable Bells:
Balangiga and Big Ben,
Great Bell of Dhammazedi,
Maria Gloriosa, St. Petersglocke,
Bells of Freedom and Liberty;
hour by hour, power of the bell tower.

Jane's Bell:
Rings with courage against the dark demon.
Sings in celebration of her patience and faith.
Clangs with durable resonance, rings and sings
and sings and rings, rung by her strong hand.

FULL SAIL

Lori Tremblay's music

The music in the wind
plays the concert of sailboats
dancing the Atlantic, off Marblehead Neck

Triangles of white
lean left, tip right
shift and drift in morning light.

Tranquil breath's pitter-patter thrum
rustles and swirls the rippling sails
stately and slow; *a minuet? Bach?*

Midday, a harder blow whips
the slap and flap of waves and wind
churns the air elusive in close-hauled sails.

Breeze strumming, waves thumping
a muscular motion, gutsy and gusty
zig-zag tacking, lurching, bucking the wind.

Boats small, smaller, near lost on the horizon
where ocean and heaven blend the same.
Something *agitato?* Something *Springsteen?*

Until the turnaround mark,
its stuttered flutter and luff
come-around full puff.

Now the downwind leg, homeward reach
spinnakers ballooned and billowed
a parade of Easter eggs on surging blue.

The right-set sail captures
and holds its air, sings, sings and sings.
Accelerando; Fortissimo; Vivaldi!

APPROACH TO DENVER

Embraced
by buckled belt
and recently remembered prayers,
I lament
the deliberate abandonment
of heaven.

Our descent
from thirty-thousand feet
is announced by the captain.

Planes approach
crisscrossed runways,
silver birds playing tic-tac-toe
in their magical reunion with earth.

Jagged peaks
stand to the West,
silhouettes, wisped by feathery blue.

Snow-capped sentries,
majestic and motionless,
they oversee the Great Plains

and in that precious heartbeat
before touchdown, my search
for angel wings...

LETTING GO

Perched atop her own Everest,
she holds on for dear life,
blond pigtails streaming
in high altitude wind.

A playmate scrambles up the ladder,
plunks down beside her, rocks forward
and joyfully squeals down the slide,
plunging into the clouds below.

Alone now, she gulps thin air,
stares beyond her outstretched legs,
hesitates in that breathless truth
between security and surrender.

Contemplating, as did Hillary and Norgay,
the traverse over Lhotse Face,
acceleration through the Khumbu Icefall,
hoped-for deceleration at base camp,

she abandons herself to gravity and
the many gods watching from the Himalayas,
slides downward to the Valley of Kathmandu,
to her mother's praise, a tolling monastery bell.

SHE FLIES

for Megan Sheehy and her family

Symbols fluttered everywhere,
like prayer flags in the Himalayas.

Old North Church was
prayerfully ribboned in blue
and all over Marblehead,
blooms of fabric, like flowers
of forget-me-not, heavenly hue.

The crop was abundant; then it fell.

But only when Megan
unfolded her young wings
and entered the skies.

Now she flies.

NAVIGATOR

Watch the October moon with me,
a rusty pumpkin slashed by the *V'd* cacophony
of flapping wings and raucous honking.

I'm curious about the Boss Goose,
the tour guide of these boisterous travelers
chasing summer, in flight patterns forever known.

Captain, at the apex of this winged wedge,
with sextant and charts, he plots celestial paths
by the same stars known to sailors, thousands of feet below.

Does his compass point to unseen threads of energy,
coalesced from earth's magnetic tug
and the spinning swirl of autumn storms?

Maybe the heavens float fading echoes
of geese now gone, beckoning their descendants
to their warm destination, like cheering fans along a marathon.

Perhaps the pilot simply squawks for *Triple A's* new map,
follows Interstate 95 South, hangs a left before reaching Savannah,
then flaps eastward to the sandy dunes of Hilton Head...

FLIGHT

in memory: Capt. Jennifer Harris,
USMC, 1978-2007

Imagine the astonished shepherd
Leaning on his staff,
Free hand shielding his eyes
Against the glare of noon,
As he scans the flapping wings
Of Daedalus and his son, Icarus,
When the younger angel,
Intoxicated by thin air,
Floats to the sun
Like a moth to light.

And in the melting,
Discards feathers and lift,
Hesitates in that fleeting truth
Between flight and gravity, then
Enters his accelerating plunge
Into the blue Aegean.

Consider our own wonder
Over the faith of flying,
When we rise above ourselves,
Praying that our wings will not fail,
Trusting our shadow below
Will keep its distance.

PERSEIDS

for Donald Mori

Comes August,
middle of the month,
shooting stars storm the night,
hold hostage the heavens.

Luminescent threads embroider
the celestial canopy, then vanish
after crisscrossing Perseus' sprinkled confetti,
shimmering against night's dark tapestry.

Comes a meteor, bold and brilliant.
Claiming an unfair share of light,
it streaks overhead then loses itself
into some omnipresent constellation.

Extinguished from sight,
it crashes into the stillness
of an unknown distant galaxy,
astonished by this entrance...

FLIGHT RISK

for Tommy

Each time I sign him out for lunch,
the attendant unlocks the door to Tommy's floor,
pats his cheek and reminds me, *he has no allowance:*
no money for a sandwich or beer or ticket for escape.

I pace myself with my friend, the shining one in school,
who could scan *Gray's Anatomy* and remember names like
parieto-occipital and *corpus callosum,* who could
memorize the map of channels and chambers that

keeps our internal trains on track and on time, and
I always return *him* on time, to this blurry destination,
which he wishes were a point of departure for
a one-way flight, a sunny landing on a straight runway.

I always sign him back in, even when I've lost him, even
when he stops mid-sentence, a lick of ice-cream dribbling
down his chin; maybe the Heath Bar Crunch I picked for him,
the list of flavors so baffling, that somewhere between

Mint Chip and Peppermint, his eyes ask for my help.
The thread's been severed, between what he's spoken
and what's still in there, like bees buzzing against
a window pane, thudding toward a bigger light.

Now his eyes are two searchlights, searching.
I see myself reflected on the dusty surface
of his eyeglasses, no deeper than that.
I don't know where he's gone,
                    and neither does he.

RESURRECTION

for Carl Scovel

Thunder on the window,
like a drumbeat on glass.
I know that sound.

On my patio the stunned robin,
fallen in a cluster of gold leaves,
wings unfolded in a limp cross,
beak thrust upward and open.
Her unblinking eye is fixed on me.

I approach, slow as a lengthening shadow,
then genuflect beside her and whisper
my finger over her feathers, stroking
the thready pulse fluttering her warmth.
I do the only thing I can do.

I pray.

In surrounding trees, a chorus of robins,
discordant in alarm, screeching in supplication.
I consider her abandonment to winter
and the dark prowling of the neighbor's cat.

I stand guard as I ponder intervention,
its confusion of cruelty and compassion.
I am still big in her eye, when she wraps herself
in newly folded wings; hops, hops, and stops.
She does the only thing she can do.

She flies.

FOR THE ANGELS, UNWINGED

Remembering 9-11

On the flaming tower,
you faced that terrible choice;
the searing orange of the inferno,
or the leap into the blue, where gravity
harshly slammed you home.

In image only, a choice of heaven or hell
when you threw yourselves into the sky,
some holding hands, some in dizzy somersault,
others reaching, arms outstretched,
like wounded eagles searching for lift.

The early flutter,
drift and wavering
of your abandoned selves,
gave way to the straightening
of your path
acceleration
gathering momentum
plunging
as if tethered
by a bungee cord
or was it an umbilical cord
snapping you back
to earth's womb
and I could not look
I turned away
from your explosion
of unbirth.

Floating through that tainted heaven,
with your life prolonged
by those frozen gasps
lasting beyond infinity;
I prayed you were loved,
I prayed you breathed pure air,
I prayed you no longer knew
that your wings had failed you.

Now, you can fly...

FAMILY

SIXTY CANDLES

for Bonnie

The candled cake
brought sweetness
and some light
to your celebration.

Sixty years of earned shadows
dance behind your smile,
comfortable
in the flickering invitation.

I watched the glittering stars
that were your granddaughters' eyes,
and the soft shining
that warmed your loved ones.

I realized:
you brought
your own light...

KRISTEN

Last minute, I raced
to Stop & Shop to
pick out a cake
for her birthday.

Chocolate, vanilla frosting,
embroidered with flowers and leaves,
red and gold with autumn's feelings.
How could she be forty?

Why didn't I special order
something with berries and sweet yogurt,
big and flat like polished marble, inscribed
with my thesaurus, my many words of love?

Squinting over her steamed glasses,
the bakery clerk asked for a name.
Her hands angling the wax-paper cone,
she swirled *Kristen* in emerald green
beneath the raspberry *Happy Birthday*.

Something about her fluid scribbling,
her frosting pen steady, never
lifting from the unbroken line
made my daughter's name a gift,
glowing in that honest light of October.

DECEMBER GIFT

for Alexa

Comes December,
tenth day of the month,
my first grandchild's birth
thaws the magnified brilliance
of the frozen northern night.

The Milky Way
festoons a halo, shimmering
beyond the hunter Orion, luminous
in pursuit of Atlas' doved daughters,
the seven stars of the Pleiades.

Pegasus' unfolded wings
reach for Ursa Major, the Great Bear,
who noses for the focused clarity
of the North Star.

My crystallized breath,
an opaque mist suspended
like a silver prayer,
smudges the glowing confetti,
constant in celestial assembly.

Just before my *Amen*,
the lucid congregation blurs,
dissolves the darkness
into a pale wash of the heavens,
glistening, warm and moist
on my cheek...

FIRST DAY OF SCHOOL

School morning,
autumn air whispers
summer's reluctant leave-taking.

Alexa shines,
eager to begin
a brave new chapter.

She shimmies
into her backpack, full
of pencils, crayons, and books.

One hand grips her lunch-boxed
peanut-butter and jelly sandwich,
guarded by Winnie-the-Pooh.

Other hand,
after a summer of playing
elusive butterfly, unwilling to be netted,
flutters to, cinches and blanches
her mommie's hand...

ANGELA'S MANTRA

I can do that!
Proclaiming her competence,
she traipses after her big sister
as if tethered by a bungee cord.

Angela follows her leader,
mimics a spinning pirouette,
wobbles a dizzy somersault,
then breathlessly puffs
"I can do that!"

Like a rolling tumbleweed,
little sister races,
chases on churning legs.

"I can do that, all by myself,"
her grin shines like noonday sun
skipping over a field of daisies.

HOW GOD LOOKS

Angela, age seven,
theologically confident
as a Biblical scholar,
told her grandmother
about God, how He looks.

Like a ball of sequins,
she said, *with*
sparkles and glitters
and darts of light,
spraying rainbows everywhere.

She has it on highest authority
that when we are born,
God gives each of us a sequin,
which grows within us, and
when we die, we are *all* sequin.

This is the gospel, according to Angela…

TEA PARTY

for Alexa and Angela

Latte, two cocoas, whipped cream on top.
Two little girls laugh with grandpop.
Flowery dresses, hair up in bows,
glittering sandals hug wiggly toes.
Raspberry jam, smudged on each face.
We are the focus of the warm coffee place.
Others, distracted by our giggling and glee,
float tolerant winks and smiles at me.
I was the eye of a jubilant storm,
which spun lightness and form
to the unweighted time of a summer day
when I felt like the star of a lovely play...

I WILL TELL MY DAUGHTER

for Kristen

When a loved father dies,
a proclamation should go forth
for all those busy men who wish
to be loved fathers.

Perhaps pealing bells from a tower in Tuscany
drifting through valleys and vineyards
echoing above blaring traffic in bustling cities
calling us busy men to attention

that we may be still
in order to contemplate
what we must do
to be loved fathers.

A carpenter holsters his hammer;
a lonely soldier leans on his rifle, studies a picture;
a writer puts down his pen and escapes his novel
long enough to remember the people in his own story.

I will tell my daughter she is more radiant
than the daylily named Stella D'oro
which blooms gold in spring, summer, and fall
because *she* shines in all seasons.

I will tell my daughter that
when I am gone she must stand
in the country church of my garden
with the congregation of flowers and attentive angels

and listen for my voice.

BREATHING OLD AIR

for my grandfather, who died in a fire
when my mother was eight years old

Grandfather, your eyes are troubled.
This parched and faded photograph,
blurred with the last year of your life,
shows eyes focused and searching.

Did you smell your approaching hell?
Old Man, was there a whiff
of the acrid flames, soon
to widow your wife?

Your eyes seem about to tear,
knowing the salty lick
ten children would taste,
my mother among them.

Is your interrogation mere curiosity
with a nosy grandson, pondering you
from the safer side
of our shared history?

Grandpa, I will sit with you
while the smoke blows away.
We'll wait for rain, soaking and cool.
We'll breathe the scrubbed freshness
                    that lingers...

ANNIVERSARY

for Bonnie

We are
a long time married,
today.

Long enough
for a tree
to grow tall,

bend
with the wind,
shed heavy rain

and feel that
the sun
is not always kind.

Long enough
for its leaves,
gone gold from green,

to be held
late into Autumn,
then released.

A new season, blessed.

AUNT MARY'S TABLE

was wooden, round and worn.
The grainy surface absorbed
spilled coffee and family history.
Its height was right
for resting elbows in conversational posture,
gently nudging bowls of pea soup and wooden trays
of firm green peppers, tangy onions, plump rosy tomatoes
from Uncle Jack's garden.

Smudged family pictures and wrinkled letters littered
our gatherings, documenting that we belonged to each other.
Aunt Mary's chair was nearest the stove,
where she could fill plates as they emptied.
Her table was a stage where laughter danced.
It was a floor where sorrow scuffed heavy steps.
Aunt Mary's table recycled sadness around its perimeter,
like a spin-dryer evaporating heaviness
from a damp garment as it circled in our discourse,
shedding weight with the touch of each cousin.

One Spring it was a pulpit, joining our blurred images
with soft prayers when our breathing was quiet,
listening for her breathing to quiet.

Soon her place at the table was empty, but not vacant.
Our family meetings did not stop; we still sipped coffee,
talked about children, and now, grandchildren.
Sometimes, we talked about the New Hampshire weather.
On warm Summer days, through the open window
we inhaled the delicate fragrance of geraniums.
In Autumn, I think it was marigolds...

ONE DAY, ONE MONTH, ONE YEAR

for the sister I never knew

Frances, it is time we talked.
Father died, but you know that.
He's been with you more than a year now;
you've been with Mother a decade and a half.

I gathered Dad's papers, checkbooks, and legal stuff.
A tattered envelope hid a harsh receipt,
and a crinkled map from Koch's funeral home.
Twenty-seven dollars was the cost of your casket,
your address, plot 9-T; but I know where you are.

If not for your unbirthday, we would have shown you
how to bait a hook, field a grounder on the big hop.
Little sister's first prom? We'd have chaperoned,
three mothers, disguised as brothers.

You'd have taught us to be less heavy afoot,
to be more nimble in our vigilant scrambling
between the hard-edged shadows of Mother's demons.

There was another paper, Frances:
a pictured pamphlet, glossy after all this time, entitled
Remember the Love of a Child, with a Matthews Memorial.
Gracefully penciled among the selections, were Mom's notes.
She emerged from her darkness long enough to underline
the bronze Angelic Style, sixteen inches by eight.

It is flat above you, Frances, weathered by sweet air
from those fertile cornfields, across Route 26.
From my side, I read the engraved silence.
The space for dates is half-used, with one inscription.
It says: July 21, 1949. It says: *She rests with the Angels.*

LAMENTATION

for my brothers

Yesterday
   The incessant creak
   of our Mother's rocking chair
   echoed in my memory's ear.
   Her swaying beat synchronized
   with shadowed songs of fear
   from voices only she could hear.

Yesterday
   My brothers and I marched with
   exquisite softness, like spiders
   traversing wispy webs in unlit corridors.
   Our cadence dutifully mimicked
   the thin drumming which accompanied
   my Mother's entrances and exits,
   her unpredictable attendance
   to our boyhood.

Yesterday
   We walked with feathery steps
   as if on crusted snow, waiting
   for the surface to let go.
   We knew the packed cold in our shoe,
   the melting, clammy wetness
   which would be a long time drying.

Yesterday
   My Mother rocked, Book of Prayers
   clutched to her breast.
   She stared through her window,
   searching for God, and she could not see
   her three sons standing in the doorway

as we waited for instructions
    about following the Shepherd,
        about the gathering of sheep...

FIREFLIES

At the end,
words no longer
touched my mother.

Embellished
by whatever velvet
my voice could muster,
my greetings, heavy
with empty weight,
plunged to the floor.

My well-meant words
became scattered noise,
unheard by her,
deafening to me.

My mother's eyes
fluttered their inquisition,
deflecting my identity
into her abandoned history.

At the end,
mystified eyes surrendered,
whispered blinking recognition,
twinkling remembered light
into our shared darkness.

I remembered fireflies...

VESPERS

Intersecting with Interstate Eighty, the road to Danville
meanders through the farmlands of Central Pennsylvania.
My journey of fifty-two years past, repeated.
My dread, disguised as an eight-year old boy, conceded.
Accompanied by my father, who could not go alone,
to visit my mother in her Purgatorial Home.

Countless trips past this turn
my mind's compass pointed here,
that I revisit this route and learn
about my Mother's frozen fear.

Columns of rigid trees stand sentry,
authorizing entry to my buried, worried history.
Dark brick buildings cluster into an edifice,
claiming an unfair share of Autumn's slate sky.

Shrouded memories clear,
as the prison-like tower appears.
The imposing fortress draws near, with
remembered music I once again hear, its
harmony and verse so empty, it could only
have been invented by souls tormented.

I remember,
passing through the dark wooden door,
my mother rocking across the stone floor,
Her bent silhouette softened
by failing afternoon light, glinting off
windows, subdivided by purposefully-attached bars.

I remember,
as the early winter sun diminished,
a murmuring chorus of unrest replenished

the dark energy of my mother's residence.
Invisible soloists sing a song of sadness.
The undirected choir hums the music of madness.

I remember,
echoes of that mantra swirling in the air
above my mother's shadowed companions,
swaying in common time, each
in their own rocking chair.

I remember,
their primitive singing, pleading
for meaningful location of their Beings.
And in the twilight above, the sound
of fluttering wings, attached to lost souls,
circling and seeking within their confused caretakers,
a familiar place of rest.

I remember,
as I rose to leave, my mother tearfully
faced me, embraced me, could not erase me
from her presence; could not release me.
The rhythmic rocking and chanting halted:
Vespers...abruptly suspended, in heavy air
until she freed me, her hopes defaulted.
The singing resumed, metered as before.
Hummed vibrations timed our steps,
as my father and I walked to the door.

I remember,
I turned to my mother and waved my hand.
My young boy's eye then saw
what my ear could not understand.
Hollow faces, unmoving mouths monotoned:
We are lost, we are lost, we are not found...

I remember.
I wanted my Mother to be Found.

SHOE SHINE

Like a parade of abandoned feet,
they stand at attention, awaiting
the Saturday shining.

My father lines up the family shoes
in tidy rows of black, brown,
mahogany purple called oxblood.

Dad daubs on the polish,
camouflaging scrapes and scuffs
earned by my brothers and me.

I march behind, in perfect step.
With soft-bristled brush,
my back and forth buffing

Lifts from leather its glow,
masking the wounded surface
in the glare of reflected light.

The sharing lures from us
our own hidden glow, glazing
the injuries within.

For that efficient hour,
my father shines in my presence,
and I in his...

ON THE CARE OF A HARDWOOD FLOOR

In our boyhood home, my brothers and I restore
the gloss of my father's floor; maple, durable, hard.
With stain, polyurethane, and sandpaper by the sheet
we've supplies enough to erase the echoed scuff
of harsh steps, in this empty house, *empty house;*
fix the floor of this empty house, *empty house.*

By the window, my mother rocked in her chair while
waiting for God, rosary-bound hands worried in her lap.
Through the grainy wood of my father's perfect floor,
the chair notched her scarred supplications, as she swayed
like a metronome, back and forth, *back and forth,*
pushed and pulled by voices only she could hear.

I sand the splintered ruts, back and forth, *back and forth,*
hard on my knees, leaning hard on the paper's sweeping scrape,
brushing the blemished surface, back and forth,
whisking away the creaky music of her solitary dance.

The wood renewed, I glide my hand, seeking healing,
back and forth, *back and forth*, feel the floor unscarred,
feel it cool and smooth as marble, then wait for approval.

Good job, whispers my father's ghost
in this empty house, *empty house,*
and my mother is at peace, *at peace.*

PRAYER, IN MY POCKET

Procrastination saved my green cotton shirt,
faded by too many washings and wearings.

Bulging the pocket was a crumpled note
which unfolded its fragile remembrance:
the grocery list for my father's final birthday.

Faded ink blurred his request for
hot dogs and rolls, pretzels and beer,
chocolate ice cream for a May afternoon
five weeks before he died.

His children and grandchildren laughed,
sang and shared tales of his ninety-six years.
Great-granddaughters cartwheeled, dancing
his determined spirit on the green grass.

When weary sun peeled back
The soft purple hills, exposing evening's blush,
my brothers and I steadied my father
into his goodbyes, which circled him
like early summer's hug.

We took him home the long way.
We bathed and pajama'd him,
tucked him in, sat on his bed.
I brushed my hand through his hair,
a full head of white, worn in all seasons
like a proudly balanced mound of snow.

Whispered blessings lingered
in the sweet Pennsylvania air,
luffing the curtains of his open window.

I was wearing my green cotton shirt,
less faded then, grocery list in the left pocket,
a prayer, softly against my heart...

ALLES IN ORDNUNG

Before my tired father went to sleep,
he asked about his children
and his grandchildren, even our pets.

Like a farmer collecting his crops,
he made a reckoning of what to keep
and what to let go.

My brother softly told him
everything is fine, Dad.
The accounting was final.

Alles in ordnung,
said my father,
then whispered *Gute nacht.*

His *good night* was hushed in the sleep
of the pale hours, when the air is still
And the darkness knows everything.

And his sons gathered his harvest.

SIMPLE WOOD

My father was durable and strong,
could bend far and not break
like simple wood.

He cared not for
embellishment or decoration.
His grain was true and good, unadorned
like simple wood.

Like a statuesque tree
he stood straight and tall.
And when I last looked at him,
he lay straight and tall, enclosed
in simple wood...

INHERITANCE

When the debts and credits
were reconciled,
when his home was sold
and the proceeds deposited
in the estate account,
when the value
of his earthly possessions
was calculated
for taxation
of his net worth,
what remained
of my father's ninety-six years
was divided equally
among his three sons…

a distribution
of thirty-two years
for each heir...

BROOM-CLEAN

Legal papers documented the terms
for selling the home my father built:
agreed-upon purchase price; proof
of no liens against his estate; and the request
to leave our boyhood home *broom-clean*.

We three brothers packaged our past
in cardboard cartons, for relocation,
or reluctant abandonment.

Through the back door, we angled
his cherry-wood table, danced it over the yard,
then cushioned it inside my brother's van.
Four matching chairs obediently followed,
like children tagging after their mother.
Wrought-iron lamps, welded by his hands,
we wrapped in heavy wool sweaters,
warm gifts of Christmas past.
We bundled pale photographs, to be aired
at future gatherings, where fresh sunlight
would illuminate the hope on my parents' faces,
smiling from the other side of our history.

Then, sweeping. From lonely bedrooms,
I spanked dirt from corners and closets.
Clustered dust, fuzzy with our past, outraced
my broom's brushed goodbyes.
Past my father's stone fireplace, into the kitchen,
I chased the growing congregation into the dustpan,
sacrificed my collected offering to a trash bag,
then tossed it by the garage door.
It collapsed homelessly, on a discarded mattress.

In my father's room, the low angle of October sun
bled the day's end against faded green walls.
Particles of escaped dust shuddered, then settled
with the hollow echo I heard, when, for the last time,
I slammed and latched the weary kitchen door...

MEDITATION ON BRASS

Each Christmas
my brothers and I
polished our tree holder,
machined by my father
from solid brass.

His mantra hummed the air,
filled our breathing.
Patience. Take your time. Do it right.

Along with the art,
I've inherited the task.
Each year I replenish the shine,
my father comes to me
with his words renewed.

Smearing on the creamy polish,
I massage the textured surface.
Patience, he sighs under my rubbing rag.

Where he burnished the metal
into the curve of a heavy chalice,
I place my hands on his hands,
spin circles on the blemished patina,
buff away the rusted days
from one Christmas to the next..
Take your time, he breathes on my fingers.

I stroke the twice-folded cloth
back and forth, up and down,
until the hazy surface
becomes a fluid glow, releasing
the sweat of my father's labor,
dormant within the brass.

You did it right, he whispers…
and I stand in his light.

WHAT I TOOK FROM MY FATHER

I wanted a different name,
like Joseph or Thomas or Michael.
Clemens sounded vaguely religious,
an uncertain closing to a prayer.

My father's name, given to me,
means mercy and understanding.
But charity was not easily embraced
when he was bent, tender from hard work.
Compassion was a blurred vision
when sweat stung his worried eyes.

Because his hands were calloused,
mine were not.
What was hard-edged in my father,
is softer in me, like a stone,
burnished in the river bed.

Now, I know my name.
It sounds vaguely religious,
like an uncertain closing to a prayer.

REFLECTIONS

SUNSET, LATE NOVEMBER

End of the afternoon walk.
Autumn's honest sky magnifies Boston,
its silhouette so close I could touch it,
burn my hand on the big sun sinking behind.

I reach Red Rock, my turnaround point,
head for home, easterly. Halfway there,
the evening sky throbs, blushed and bruised
in its purple battle with sunset.

Even the ocean's a flamboyant participant.
The outgoing tide, a rippling wash of wine,
something red, something pale burgundy,
the sand stained by it.

I turn back to the conflagration in the west,
the Boston skyline, a burnt barcode in a rose fire.
Thin clouds slice the incandescence like gold daggers,
bleeding the horizon into a bigger redness.

I climb our hill, stopping, turning, backward stumbling.
There's fire in the sky behind me, fire in front of me,
the reflection of a hundred west-facing windows
flaming, as if each house is burning inside.

VENUS AND THE WAXING MOON

Following the report of numbers in Iraq,
politics, and the shortstop's strained achilles,
the weatherman on the 6 o'clock news
directs my eye to the western sky.

Balanced on the roof of my neighbor's house,
the moon's crescent curls its amber horn,
flirting with Venus, a jewel poised on the chimney,
glittering through the pale fading of day.

By eight o'clock, the bawdy pair
dangles from my pine tree, glaring
like gold ornaments, floating
on the purpled cobalt of night.

Just before 10, the lunar sliver unfurls
its lusty burning, gaining on the Goddess,
radiant in her attraction of celestial companions,
trapped in the deception of their separate orbits...

PIETA

Forgive my unbelief.
Until I faced that shining stone,
I took Michelangelo at his word:

A block of marble, from Carrara.
Its flash, sparkle, and gleam
most perfect he'd ever worked.

I believed that it was inert;
that it passively yielded itself
to the artist's hands and vision.

Until I stood before the crucified Jesus,
lowered and layered across Mary's lap;
until I saw his twitching tendons

and felt the cooling glow
of life leaving his limbs,
I'd believed in cold stone.

Forgive now, my unbelief.
His muscles, stretched and strained,
flared ribs beneath translucent skin?

And Mary's contemplative grief
does not explain her glistening eyes
if she came from *a block of marble.*

Did it not flinch
with each chiseled tap
of the sculptor's mallet?

NO SHOW

My guest is late.

The table is dressed with napkins and fine linen.
My good china is rimmed by polished silver, glinting
like the tall candle flickering at the cut flowers.
I sacrificed the best blooms of my white and gold lilies;
some slender delphinium spikes, cobalt-blue.

Red wine, robust, berry overtones, a winner from Argentina,
has been uncorked and is breathing, and so have I, at least
been opened and breathing, or maybe sighing.
My guest is very late.

I was hoping for a little time, one on one,
perhaps some thoughtful conversation about that sunrise
at Pemaquid Light; possibly some words to paint
that indescribable rose sun, floating like a balloon
over the purple mist.

I'd like some guidance about the last line of a love poem,
so as to curb my tendency to finish with spongy syllables,
syrupy, overly sentimental, mushy, or maybe squishy?

Now it's really late. I'll just step out on the porch,
give a quick look up and down the street.
Guess I'll pour a glass and turn off the roast.

The invitation was timely, so neatly inked,
exquisite penmanship on heavy parchment;
properly addressed, I might add.

Dear Muse, it began...

NO SUMMER POEM

The long drought
has dried up my writer's pen,
replaced it with my sharp-bladed shovel,
its thwack-uh thwack-uh trochaic chopping
splitting the baked soil from my parched flowers.

I water and soothe my plants
with the unforced meter of pastel words,
before edging the line breaks between
purple-spiked ajuga and pink buds of geranium.
Enjambment blurs the imagery.

Revision is the annual in my garden of perennials.
This summer I clustered my peonies and lilies in threes,
tercets of coral red and boastful gold, standing watch over
a daylily named Ice Carnival, a pure soul misted with lime,
so ethereal it blooms like an angel holding its breath.

I've finally given in to center-justification
for the glaring white shasta daisy, so tall
it claims an unfair share of sunlight as it
benevolently gazes down on its neighbors.
It must think it's a simile, behaving like a king.

The editing never ends, cutting and culling.
I am the harsh executioner, who deliberates
and decides what to replant and what to uproot.

Is there no end to killing my precious darlings?

SILLY SONNET

Writing a sonnet is a daunting task
with guidelines to pace the writer's timing.
Sometimes it seems too much to ask
for fourteen lines with proper rhyming.

It's not such a trial to write free verse
but this is a rather tricky assignment.
I find the rhyme, then work in reverse
to place the words in proper alignment.

The rhythmic beat controls the meter,
releasing words the poem has spoken.
I follow commandments to please the reader,
but sometimes rules are made to be broken.

It seems a sonnet tests the poet.
I'm not sure, but I think I've blown it!

SENTENCE

Fluttering wings of ebony
blacken my dream.
Beady eyes knife my soul.

The Crow has stolen
my shiny pen, and with it,
my poem.

A dark-robed judge
in a dead birch tree,
he presides over my fate.

He folds his shadowed feathers,
wraps himself
in the dark night of his plumage.

He is judge and jury,
harsh captor of my muse.
Raucously, he mocks my supplication.

"When will I have my pen?"
He is Poe's Raven
and he taunts me.

"Nevermore!"

CUP OF COFFEE

I forgot her question.
Bewitched, bewildered, or both
by the pale glow of her eyes,
I was busy returning the smile
of the counter girl at Starbucks.

> *Some sort of blue, her eyes...*
> *as if diluted by a wash of moonlight.*
> *Perhaps a hint of turquoise,*
> *how it tints the Caribbean hue*
> *of Rendezvous Bay in, let's see...*
> *I believe it was Virgin Gorda,*
> *no, maybe Anguilla, um,*
> *yes it was definitely Anguilla*
> *where the morning light breathes*
> *blue into the sky, leaving a mist*
> *like glittering diamonds on blue water,*
> *such a pale blue, so beguiling, so...*

Sir! Excuse me Sir! May I help you?

Oh! Yes. Sorry. Latte. Tall.

> *like a drop of blue ink,*
> *how it unfolds into summer*
> *in a glass of clear water, how,*
> *when you lift it to the sun*
> *you hold endless sky in hand,*
> *you see through clouds and stars*
> *a far-reaching galaxy of blue, lighter*
> *than cobalt or indigo or peacock,*
> *cornflower, forget-me-not blue, almost...*

> Sir, your change. Don't forget your change!

NAMES OF STARS

What do you name when you search the heavens?
The evening glare of Venus? The glow of the Milky Way,
the Hercules Cluster, faintly visible to the naked eye?

Hold open your chart; identify the brilliant occupants of night,
the vigilant guards and migrating refugees of the darkness:
Aldebaran, the bloodshot eye of Taurus; Antares, heart of Scorpion;
the pulsing variable, Delta Scuti, blinking like a firefly on a summer night.
Do you bow to the nuclear angels, Giansar, Rastaban, Thuban,
potent in light, holy in name?

What might we see from those distant galaxies,
telescope reversed, our vision directed toward earth?
Are *we* not stars in our own constellations?

Find our names in temples and mosques, churches and choirs,
nursing homes and prisons. Search for the teacher of children,
the grass mower, the sweating young man on the trash truck,
the driver of the eighteen-wheeler on the endless interstate,
the healer of the spirit, the one who sutures the bleeding wound.

We move in our own elliptical orbits, responding
to the gravity between us, trying to get it right, between us.
We carry our own sacred light; *our* names are celestial.

Hold open your chart. Name the congregation:
    Abdul, Bhudevi and Charlie, Dennis, Florence, Giovanni,
    Heather and Itzak, Jean, Kareem, Megan and Ming,
    Santiago, Sophia, Tomas and Tim, Yakez and Zackary.

From A to Z, each of us carries our own *Holy of Holies.*
    Name yours. Be blessed by it.

NAMES OF DAYLILIES

I'm at my table by the window,
morning sun reflecting a harsh glare
from my uncluttered blank page.
I'm trying to write a poem.

Too many distractions:
the boastful cardinal perched in my Red-Bud tree,
yodeling its fluid legato, rising and falling staccato;
the distant thrash of waves, buffeting Egg Rock.

Most of all, the luminous congregation of Daylilies
gathered in the purple-blue vase, glazed
by a pale smearing of white and rose clouds.
The alchemy of *Stella D'oro* transforms light to gold.
Raspberry-wine *Pardon Me,* rudely demands
my attention, as if speaking its own name.
I pick up my pencil, but it ends up nicked,
clenched between my teeth, when
Tender Love winks its ivory eye, caressed
by blossoms of flesh-pink petals.

Give me a break! Even my pen's blue ink
pales in the cobalt blue of Delphinium spikes,
flaring between the fireworks of *Bashful's*
dark crimson, yellow-throated torch song
and I cannot write a single word.

NOVEMBER GRAY

There's something about November Gray.
Leafless, skeletoned trees are bare,
fragments of summer swept away,
while frozen promises clutch the air.

November teaches me to Pray.

Something about a November Day,
its deliberate, colorless retreat
from sparkling skies, unweighted play.
My faith tested; will summer repeat?

November teaches me to Pray.

VITREOUS HUMOUR

the clear gel that fills the eye

Flecks of free-floating collagen
cruise the ocean of my eye,
tiny sailboats with squiggly lines,

sails puffy, curved and full-blown.
An optical hallucination for some.
Floaters, a vision test for my muse:

a strand of cobweb, unraveled, playing
hide-and-seek with my inquisitive gaze;
a long-tailed pollywog, darting

to the periphery of my vision when
I focus on what can't be focused on;
a blurred comet, flashing its tail

across my darkness, when I'm angled
toward something bright in the night;
a spermatozoon thrashing *its* tail,

desperate in its futile search
for a welcoming egg,
lost in the wrong ocean.

LOST, IN INNER SPACE

Trekking the Himalayan terrain
of my vast cerebral cortex,
I tumbled down a slippery crevasse
between mountainous folds of gray matter.

The valley below was littered with notes
inked in red or scribbled with lead.
  pound of regular, half of decaf
  shirts to laundry, light on the starch
  dental appointment, Tuesday at Two.

So this is where lost reminders go,
those cues to remember this errand or that!
Here they shed their camouflage, blend
in our puffing, catch your breath breathing
which blows away thoughts, once fixed in the mind.
  Real Estate taxes, end of the month
  library book, one month overdue
  big anniversary, get a nice card.

Synaptic humming of dutiful neurons
proves memory loss is just an illusion.
It's all stored away, inside my brain,
accessible, if I could just remember...

TURTLE

Slow moving and squat,
encased
in his protective memory,
he hauls
his own darkness.

When light glares
as a hurtful shining,
he is diminished

into his known night...

DREAMCATCHER

When our baseball gloves wore out,
we passed them down, brother to brother.

Being the oldest, I was first to wear one new:
the *J.C. Higgins Model 1623,* from Sears.

For more than a game of catch,
our mitts got us into the sunshine,

away from the extra innings of darkness clouding
my mother's unwinnable game with her demons.

Nightly I nurtured my glove with the ritual rub of
Neetsfoot, replenishing the skin, restoring the pulse

and breath of the living hand on my hand, then put it
to bed beneath my bed, ball tucked within the glove

like a child asleep, dreaming of the leaping catch,
the sure-handed scoop of the skittering grounder

starting the choreographed relay of a double-play,
thunder-throbbing cheers in Yankee Stadium.

With dutiful repetition, I thumped the mitt with my fist,
molding the leathered palm into a sweet spot

between first finger and thumb, the pocket
in which the caught ball stays caught.

The heart, which allows no loss.

NOT VITRUVIAN MAN

Da Vinci sketched his man
with arms and legs flared
in perfect symmetry, his wingspan
a stretched circle, boxed in a square.

Bilaterally mirrored on each side,
paired muscles flex and brace,
propelling movement and easy glide,
upright posture and unforced grace.

Hah! Leonardo's perfect guy
didn't have it so rough—
he wouldn't fly so high
with a torn rotator cuff!

No fun getting older;
can't do a thing
with a bum shoulder
and the wing in a sling.

RECESS AT MACHON ELEMENTARY

Troops of kindergartners
invade and conquer
the school playground.

Camouflaged in jackets
green, red, and blue,
yellow sweaters
purpled with flowers,
they ricochet in their attack,
like a sleeting of jellybeans.

Playmates confiscate
ladders, swings, and slides.
Others flutter in clusters
like skittish butterflies,
then shudder in their landing.
They rise and fall, lift and land,
relentless in their dizzy dance.

Just before the clanging close
of this jubilant bubbling,
a squealing of boys gasps by,
pursued by a missile named Shauna.
Her arms and legs churn circles,
as she abandons her cherub face
in pursuit of justice, blond hair
blurred and long behind her,
while other pink-faced tormenters
catch their breath,
   chagrined and tumbled
          in her wake....

MEMORIAL DAY

The holiday traffic is heavy but humming on I-84, in brisk cadence
with Brandenburg Concerto#1. We cross the Hudson, head for Boston.
Soon we slow, lurch, and creep. We stop, start, stop. Turn engines off.
I push *eject* and Bach emerges on a silver platter.

Funny faces from two small boys in the Volvo ahead.
We lower the windows for a breeze and next to us
the tank-topped SUV driver flaps his tatooed arm.
Is late... gonna be late for Manuel's birthday. Damn!
From her Beetle, a young alto sings with the Beatles,
harmonizing with Paul or George, *let it be, le-et-it be.*
Two middle-aged jocks, pot-bellied in a Silver Convertible,
high-five over news of the Red Sox thumping the Yankees.

Then comes the approaching wail of sirens, layering
discordant harmony on the interrupted holiday morning.
We squeeze left, an inch, a foot, *a prayer.* Police, fire truck,
two rescue vans and a tow truck bully the breakdown lane.
The blue and red flashing pulls away, sinks below the horizon
like a failed sunrise. The sound hangs hard in heavy air.
Drivers step out, stand at attention, scan the distance
like sentries, and I must remember to breathe.

Then, a nudging of cars in the distance. Doors close respectfully.
Hushed engines cough and sputter into a murmured hymn.
The cars slip forward, funnel with alternating courtesy into single file.
The procession whispers past the scene, and I cannot look, but I look
at the skid marks, black and breathing, scribing the long and graceful arc,
left side of the highway to the right, curved sweep of an angel's wing.

Purple cornflowers and Queen Anne's Lace, toppled and tangled
in the mangled guardrail, where the path flows over the embankment.
We ease past firemen and policemen and EMTs, quietly tall, bowed
in a bent staring, and it doesn't matter about the Red Sox and Yankees;

the Beatles will sing again, and the SUV man's left arm is muscled
quietly against the car door and he would be late for Manuel's party
and it would be OK.

You know the truth of this by the young fireman staring downward,
how his tan uniform with yellow stripes bends his proud posture,
left arm akimbo, helmet clasped under the right, braced against his hip.
And the one thing you feel in your breathing and in your heart is that
                                        these things do not matter.

MEA MAXIMA CULPA

Mea culpa, through my fault...

With the Latin of my altar boy days
I chant my plea for pardon.
In your hour of need, I abandoned you.
My own distractions, in front of me
like paintings on a gallery wall,
draw me away, annul my devotion to you.

Mea culpa, through my fault...

Your puzzled gaze burns its inquisition
like a branding iron, singeing my heart
with a smoldering *Why?*
You looked to me for nurturance;
but the cup was empty.
You stood before me, face uplifted.
I did not touch you.

Mea maxima culpa,
          through my most grievous fault...

When I immersed my guilt
in the brown sweetness of your eyes,
when I caressed the surrendered droop
of your velvet-black ears, then
rattled the forgotten *Kibbles and Bits*
into your barren bowl,
the sweeping swish of your tail whispered,
     I forgive you,
               I forgive you,
                         I forgive you.

DIAGNOSIS

remembering April, 1996

Friday afternoon. My doctor's stethoscope, like Beethoven's hearing-horn, questioning my chest. The music was not good. His nurse took some blood. I waited in his private office. From his desk, his wife and children smiled at me from a sunny rim of the Grand Canyon, confined within an 8 x 10 wooden frame. My doctor entered. Closed the door. He sat across from me, sliding his chair close. Leaned in, elbows heavy on the table, eyes worried. Eyes really worried. He was now my dear friend of twenty years, the doctor faded into the diplomas behind him. *Your Platelets. Low. Dangerously low.* I asked for the truth. *Maybe nothing or maybe... Leukemia.* He sent me to the Cancer Center, he'd already called. In my car I was driver *and* passenger. One of us concentrated on driving so the other could worry. When I arrived three doctors were waiting. They examined me, looked for signs of bleeding, magnified my blood under the microscope. Detectives searching for clues. They huddled together. I waited for hours, alone in the room. Within minutes they returned, cautiously optimistic. Antibiotics for my pneumonia, steroids for my blood. Come back Monday. That's the day they draw bone marrow. *If your blood is not better we will have to draw bone marrow.* On Monday.

Friday night I was optimistic. Slept well. Saturday, busy with errands, busy with work on my house. Busy. Sunday morning, church; busy with prayers. By afternoon, more quiet than busy. Then quiet. Sunday night I slept poorly. I remembered abundant blessings. Prayed for grace and one more blessing. Monday morning the clock dispensed its minutes with deliberate reluctance. I drove to the Cancer Center, my wife's hand on my shoulder. I still feel it, her hand on my shoulder. My daughter and her two little girls were waiting. Hugged me in the cold April rain. *Pop-Pop,* they called me. It shivered me. Bonnie and I entered the warm building, both freezing in the doctor's office. The kind nurse took my blood. Everyone so kind. Soon the doctors came in. Smiling. Improvement. Progress. My immune system had been confused after invasion by two sneaky bouts of pneumonia, less than a month apart. My blood cells were at war with each other. The platelets were outflanked and ambushed, resulting in a diagnosis which sounds of distressed metre:

Idiopathic Thrombocytopenic Purpura. ITP is easier. I *would* get better. My wife and I walked to the car in the rain. It was a soft refreshing rain, gentle and nurturant, good for flowers and other blooming.

It did not shiver me.

OLD DOG

Now she moves in contemplation,
her vision more remembered than present.
This time is good for her, early summer, warm.

She must understand the 23rd Psalm, its green meadows,
the way she flops down on tender grass, the black hulk of her
like an anchored boat, nosing into delicious wind.

She ignores the repetitive chime of the ice-cream truck,
but twitches her ears, loving the cardinal's aria,
two notes, legato, the rising and falling staccato.

In soft rain, she rests on her haunches,
Brooding Buddha in meditation. I call to her.
Calli. Come! Don't you know to come in from the rain?

Through her brown, cloudy eyes, she considers me.
I must look like one of Monet's cataracted angels,
smudged halo and blurry light.

She grants acceptance of my narrow understanding, moves
that part of her which will be last to die, her wagging tail.
As if to say, *I am becoming the rain...*

FOURTEEN ANGELS

I'm on my back with morning calisthenics, while
my black Lab and I listen to Segovia's classical guitar.
We are waiting for the phone to ring.

Calli usually nudges me for strokes or a belly-rub.
But with this morning's sad distance between us,
she stretches away, head heavy on her paws, as if

contemplating the great outdoors, dreaming the
heaven of green pastures and shadowed valleys.
We are waiting for the phone to ring.

Now Segovia plays *The Evening Song*
from Hansel and Gretel, and I remember
my first grade play at Pine Grove Elementary.

I was Hansel, my thin voice singing
  when at night, I go to sleep,
  fourteen angels watch do keep...

I cover my face and weep.
My sobbing lifts Callie from her reverie.
She struggles up, lurches and hobbles to me.

With her big head against my chest,
she pushes me flat onto the slate floor,
licks my face, loves the salt of my tears.

The phone rings; he's on his way. Our wait is over.
Soon we hug this dog, bury ourselves in her blackness.
The kind veterinarian kneels by her soft bed.

I beckon the angels.

A SIMPLICITY

Last night's snowfall
brought a bending,
a white humbling, to the
tall pines out back.

I know that posture,
standing proud, then
bowed, like those
tall pines out back.

Some burdens build
and weigh heavy,
like gravity's pull on the
tall pines out back.

Sun shines and melts the snow,
brings a white shedding,
a noble unbending, of those
tall pines out back.

REFLECTION

My father taught me to shave, carefully looking
upon the glass for visual guidance in gliding my
razor through the soft whiskers of my tender face.
Take your time or you'll cut and bleed, he warned.
Now I'm 80, and my daily ritual has changed.
That man in the glass now stares at me, searching.

Each morning we check each other out,
his mirrored face lathered, but not feeling
what I feel, from where I stand and stare.
I still use a brush to froth the soap, and caress
my cheeks and chin with soothing, warm bubbles.
I take my time and it feels good.

It wasn't always this way, this eye-to-eye contemplation.
For a long time in our marriage my wife would ask of me
give me your eyes, when our conversation might reveal
I was not the perfect boy my mother prayed for, not
the priest she so fervently wanted. For a long time, I
looked only at the beard of the man being shaved.

This morning the other guy in the glass smiled at me.
I saw that he had blue eyes, kind eyes. He felt good
because last night on the radio, he heard Dylan singing
Forever Young, praying that God bless and keep me,
singing of a ladder to the stars, that I climb every rung
and remain forever young; and the guy with blue eyes
                                                    blurs.

ON THE DEATH OF T-SHIRTS

Faded by too many washings and too many wearings,
My T-shirts convalesce in the bottom of my drawer.

Judge and Jury, I dispense harsh justice.
I bought them, I wore them, and now I condemn them.

Sagging silhouette of Lone Mountain's alpenglow,
Pinkly etched on the purple Montana night,
You will buff the blue hue of my van.

Turquoise shimmer of the bay in Anguilla,
And Jo-Jo the Dolphin, from the Island of Provo,
May you wipe and shine my dining room window.

Those marathon shirts, with races and places
Blurred with sweat over miles I have run,
You'll polish my shoes; I'll keep you indoors.

For now, big birthdays are given a stay...
Frayed edges and fabric, stretched like thin skin,
No longer taut, a slight slack slump to the fit,
Unraveled seams, a thread, a fiber,
one tender torn tendon at a time...

There is a vague familiarity that intervenes.

COLLECTED COINS

Glowing like a silver dollar,
the moon basks, low
on the eastern horizon.

Lifting overhead, it shrinks
into a tarnished quarter,
clinks through the hush
of prosperous constellations.

Like a bronzed nickel,
it pales toward morning,
dwindles from the jingle of stars,
        night's pocket change...

SMALL BLESSINGS AND THE 6 O'CLOCK NEWS

Here is the summary of the day's news:

Last night, firefighters led elderly residents to safety
during a smoky kitchen fire at the Jacob's Ladder Rest Home.
For the outstretched hand, seeking to be grasped,
for the hand that steadies the lame walker,
I fold mine in praise.

The Pentagon announced the latest casualty in Afghanistan,
a young father from Massachusetts, who will arrive later today
at Pease Air National Guard Base.
For the numb widow waiting on the ground,
her returning soldier high over the Atlantic,
young and cold in wooden flight, lift her
into luminous light.

Icy roads and excessive speed claimed the life of a teenage star.
All-conference quarterback and an outstanding scholar, he would
have entered Dartmouth this fall.
For the congregation of classmates, weeping
by the scarred road, pictures and roses
on a white cross; dry their salty tears, Lord.
Rub sunshine on their cheeks.

Here is a sweet video of a reunion between a young mother and
her daughter, a toddler who wandered away and was briefly lost.
For the baby girl wobbling early steps, arms flailing
toward her kneeling mother, keep them in the holiness
of each other's durable hug; let them always be large
in each other's sight.

It's that time of the year again. This weekend, Symphony Hall
will host the B.S.O. and the Handel-Haydn Chorus with their
annual performance of "Messiah."

For music, resonating in the heart, like the deep thrum
of the cello; for escaped hallelujahs, sung and unsung,
I offer my three-fold Amen.

After the commercial break, stay tuned for tomorrow's weather.

PEACE

The poet Rumi teaches us
the human condition is a *Guest House.*
Welcome each new arrival, he says—
awareness comes as an unexpected visitor.

And so I invite you in from the cold night.
Let's shake the snow from your soggy coat,
drape it over the wooden chair I've dragged
from the dining room to the fireplace.

My easy chair is yours; it's called *Lazy Boy.*
That lever on your right—push it down,
your legs will rise as you slowly recline.
The warmth will be good on your feet.

Hot tea? A cup from my Wassailing bowl?
We'll dim the lights, open the curtains
and be amazed by the miracle outside, the
winter storm diminished now, moon flickering

its blessing of light on each shimmering flake
falling from the heavens, chorus of silent hallelujahs
held in the breath of unspoken prayers, and I am
aware of this peace; aware, and I give thanks.

PEOPLE & PLACES

FRANK, WHO HAS AN EYE FOR ANGELS,

for Frank Marean

searches for those
whose plumage folds
in sacred wings.

Familiar with
his own clouds,
he seeks available light

that he may find
his path
into that shining

and on his journey,
collects coats for
those cold in winter,

brings Thanksgiving
for the homeless;
gathers groceries

for the woman, abandoned.
He knows the need
of flowers for light,

and in that truth, blooms.

WHITE CROSSES

Shadowing the Gallatin River,
Montana Route 191
uncoils in its treacherous climb
to the high mountain at Big Sky.

The ice-glazed moon
washes light on pale-blue snow,
outlining the horizon's rocky border,
jagged against the cobalt clarity of night.

Guarding the twisted road,
lofty pines stand erect,
soldiers at attention,
leery of Orion's glittering sword.

At the side of the road,
my car's headlights
flash on white crosses,
glowing and growing
as they come at me,
some alone,
others in pairs,
a cluster of four;
luminous *T's*
marking the call of *Time*
before gliding by,
lost in darkness, lost
in the night behind me...

ANGUILLA CEMETERY

The tide folds and unfolds
its turquoise drumming,
silvers a glistening lace
on the sands of Mead Bay.

Its rhythm inhales and exhales
a kind of moving breath,
rustles a ghost of lavender
in this place of interrupted dreams.

Scattered like pickup sticks,
bleached coffins lie in repose,
as if tranquilized
by Caribbean light.

Clouds billow like wedding gowns,
blush into marriage with the setting sun.
The tiniest grave, a dollhouse cathedral,
faces east in search of each new day.

Her epitaph glows, bronzed
by the low angle of falling light.
Mary is advised,
 Sleep on, Beloved...

SATURDAY MORNING AT THE TILTON DINER

Walk into the clatter of platters,
sizzling with sausage, crispy bacon, three-egg omelets.
Stroll by the kitchen where the chef barks out orders
for Linda or Robin, Penny, Dianne, the cheerful buzz
punctuated by the juke-boxed thumping
of *Splish, splash, I was takin' a bath.*

Families wedge into booths, opposing sides
slicing blueberry pancakes, bathing the incision
with maple syrup, after glazing the bronzed skin
with butter, which melts into its transparent indulgence.
Children smile through jelly-smudged cheeks,
starting a weekend with mom and dad.

At the far end of the counter, an old man
protects his coffee with the tired hunch of sad weight.
The bustling waitress screeches to a halt, tops off his cup.
She pats his cheek, whispers a smile onto his face.
He lifts up a little, like a pine tree shedding snow.

I smile at my steaming cup of coffee,
magically filled and never drained in the
scrumptious hub-bub of the Tilton Diner.

BLACK ALTAR

Vietnam memorial

Strewn along the wall are
offerings of mixed blessings:
birthday cards, notes and photos;

combat boots and 6-packs;
a long letter under a name with
no forwarding address.

A mother and father rub
their son's engraved identity
onto paper, sacred as holy parchment.

About to enter a new marriage,
a widow slides off her faded ring, tucks it
into grass, never lost, never found.

A wheel-chaired vet searches and finds,
then places flowers, blazing orange
like the bouquet of bullets

searing the night at Quang Tri,
when his buddy entered the wall,
his place now sacred with the others

on the long roll call, each name
a brief life flashing by like fireflies
in the endless night of black granite.

'NAM EYES

Jimmy, George and Rob
guard a strange sharing in their eyes.
When they give voice to it,
they call it 'nam.

Jimmy came back, different and distant,
his southern boy spirit killed by the Cong.
Submerged in his cushioned chair,
he hugs himself like a frozen statue,
knowing the thaw will kill him.

Behind dark glasses, George leaks tears.
Unable to confront the stare
of concerned inquisition, he uncovers his eyes
only for nightly attacks of napalm
and dreams of cleansing flames.

Rob tiptoes in clouds
murky with grass and gin.
Women and children scurry
from the aim of his M-16,
fall lifeless, their screams forever alive
in staccato echoes of his remembering.

Jimmy, George and Rob
have eyes that go deep,
eyes that soften in pale light,
stay a long time open, searching and
vigilant against what they already know.

ROY CORRENTI'S LIGHT

for the Vietnam Vet
who saved others

Through his telescope and faith,
Gallileo verified that light
Is celestially arranged
Around a stationary Sun.

According to laws of physics
And complexities of math,
Light travels in a straight line.
It dims far from its source, and
When passed through a prism,
Forms a rainbow.

Roy Correnti's Light is not governed
By this science; it curves and bends.
If your dark corners are known to him,
They will be illuminated.

When obscured by his known clouds,
His light *will* emerge, intense, unflickering,
Like the crescent moon, silver and hanging,
An ornament in the Christmas sky.
His is a mother light, kindling other candles.
He is a prism. He stands in his own rainbow.

HOW HE LISTENS

for Daniel Wistran

Dan's stethoscope
tethers my heart
to his vigilant ear.
He is Doctor Beethoven,
hearing horn at my chest,
probing the stretched sound
of a violin string, too tightly wound.

He leans toward me, contemplates
the tympanic drumming
of his fingers on my back.
He's in a meditation, a mantra
of voices of teachers
past and present.

I think he can hear
the celestial whoosh
of a shooting star
threading its glowing tail
through Orion's soul.
Can he hear sunset's alchemy,
the fading silver of day
blushing into evening's gold?

He attends like Robert Frost,
ear keen for flowing meter,
the beat in rhythmic accent,
the just-right rhyming of it all.

He heals me,
how he listens.
Listens, with *his* heart...

HE WAS IN MY WAY

Spare change Sir? For a sandwich?
His eyes went for mine,
a soft inquisition.
But I walked by,
as if circling a puddle.

His hunched posture
cast a thin shadow
on the sunny Boston street.
Lines etched a hard story
on his ruddy brow.

I remembered a friend's story
about the face of God, present
in all the paths we walk, where,
in selfish light, we hardly notice
the least among us.

Whether moved by guilt,
or lightly carried
by disturbed air of
a distant angel's wing,
I came back to him.

God bless you sir!
His hands cupped my folded dollar.
His face, and mine, transformed.
Who gave the blessing?
Who was least among us?

ON THE DEATH OF PETER SHECKMAN'S SON

My friend crossed the street,
then walked toward me.
I told him I was sorry for
what he was going through.

He looked at me with eyes
that could not yet release tears,
eyes that reflected the loss
of his young son's years.

He whispered *thank you*,
his posture surrendered
to the combined burden
of his own years lived,
and his child's years stolen.

The arithmetic of grief
multiplies
as it takes away...

CLASSIC SHOE SHINE, $3.00

for Weldon Bishop

Wheeled suitcase in tow,
the weary traveler shuffles to Weldon's stand,
slumps up the steps, droops himself
in the wooden chair and surrenders.

Weldon folds and tosses his Boston Globe,
lifts himself to casual attention, tilts an easy greeting.
He contemplates his calling, his priesthood of
redemption and resurrection, bows his head and steps in.

He baptizes the lifeless footwear,
spraying and wiping with his bottle of cleaner,
smears on the healing polish, caresses scars and bruises,
then rims the heel and edge of the sole
with a darker stain, as if framing a picture.
In bent homage, he hunches over the inverted *U*
of his buffing rag, arms stroking like pistons,
up and down, back and forth, pulling available light
to the glowing shoes, now beaming in renewal.
The healer steps back, darts in with a touch up rub,
as if dispersing a blemish from a forgiven soul.

The grateful king descends his throne,
folds a five into Weldon's hand, moves through the air
toward Gate 22, where he will continue his ascent on Delta,
wheeled suitcase now floating behind...

PARKINSON'S

for Dan and Ephraim

The Uninvited has found you,
trapped you in its rigid embrace.
May you walk from it, be welcomed
in a celebration of sunlight, shining
with daisies, cathedrals of lupine,
purple spikes lifting light to you.
May you glow in it.

And when your balance
tilts you and wobbles your step,
may you dance with it and
waltz to your own cadence
in steps of your own invention.
May you go with it.

May your tremor, when it comes,
cause great quaking in your demons,
topple all obstacles in your path.
May it ripple the water.
May you surf the wave's crest.
May you flow with it.

LOONS

Summer morning at Spectacle Pond.
We're on our beach chairs,
toes wiggling in warm sand.

Before my swim
I unfold *The Boston Globe,*
hold it like a shield against the sun.
I've soon abandoned myself
in the darkness of the day's news:
wars rolling downhill of their own momentum;
a child shadowed in the pale light of an Amber Alert;
Red Sox and stock market, slipping and sliding together.

I am rescued from this whirlpool of gloom
when my wife nudges me into the present moment.
Shhh...they're here...don't startle them...

I quietly lower my curtain of words.
In front of me, silhouetted by incoming light,
a pair of loons floating low on the water.
Side by side they glide, muscular necks flexed,
red eyes alert in their black heads, checkered wings
folded and curved, feathered against their sides.
The pond is a blue mirror of sky on water,
each loon a heavenly reflection of itself.

As if on cue, they dip their heads and enter the pond,
each disappearing into itself, the real and the image,
into water, into sky.

A FEW MORE YEARS

for Paul Johnson

What if I stop answering Reveille
and the wake-up music mellows,
invites me to dream in the soft warmth
of my comforter, as morning light
tip-toes into my bedroom?
Suppose I linger and sip coffee in bed,
as my wife and I
plan an unplanned day,
or unplan a planned day?

And if I plant new flowers
or nurture old flowers
or be a child
in the unpredictable company
of children,
 what about a few more years?

It is strange mathematics
that measures these *few more years*.
Does adding subtract?
Does subtracting add?

And the Accountant
on whose ledger is entered
the coming and going
of stars that glitter in the night...
He asks about net worth...

ALLEN STREET, SOUTHBOUND

Like a movie's slow sad ending,
the Nittany Theatre's closed,
replaced by The Gap.

They've fled the village, those Cowboys and Indians,
who scattered the screen with justice and dust,
rippling the dark with war-cries and shots.

Where have they gone, Roy Rogers and Hopalong;
are they faded blue ghosts in Calvin Klein jeans?
Gene Autry and Champion, trapped in The Gap,

draped in racks of T-shirts and slacks?
Lone Ranger and Tonto must have escaped
to the prosperous daylight of Allen Street, then

spurred Silver and Scout hard to the right
past Smith's Barbershop with its Vitalis musk,
scurried by the brick of The People's Bank and

the cataracted windows of McLanahan's Drugs.
They galloped south, to the outskirts of town
to the flat freedom of wheat fields and corn,

where the rising theatre of mountains and hills
echoed clopping hoofs and the resonant shout,
Hi Ho Silver, Away!

BAGGAGE CLAIM

My baggage has recycled
through many transformations,
circled patiently 'round the carousel
awaiting my recognition and rescue
from the weary march of toppled suitcases,
tipsy duffle bags, and bruised boxes.

Stretched thready at the seams, it bulged
with the weight of my mother's dark shadows,
my shoulder abraded by the downward pull
of the frayed carrying strap, my tether
to my young boy's resentment in
trying to carry what I could not carry.

Now my baggage rolls smoothly
on the wheels of acceptance and gratitude,
pulled by a handle short enough
to be close to what must be remembered,
long enough to allow—dare I say it?—
graceful posture in the pulling.

The enclosed notice informs:
This bag has been inspected.
Opening it released darkness,
replacing it with light
thus accounting for
its diminished weight.

The official jargon further explains:
Love is governed by a different gravity.
It is like feathers and cannot be weighed
All that remains in this bag is good stuff.
It can be classified as "Carry-on."
    Have a good rest of your trip.

CITIZEN YURI

for Yuri Shamritsly

This one day,
    my friend stood before me,
    taller than the day before.
    His eyes shined like meteors.
    He was lifted, an eagle floating
    on rising clouds.

Years before this one day,
    he left Russia for the echo
    of freedom ringing
    on purple mountains' majesty,
    fresh winds blowing
    on amber waves of grain.

This one day,
    he answered questions put to him
    about the Declaration of Independence, the
    Bill of Rights, affirming his embrace of our
    Constitution, thus exchanging Czars and Rulers
    for Presidents and Senators.

This one day,
    the twenty-third of June, last year of this millennium,
    I understood what I had taken for granted
    when my friend Yuri proclaimed,
    "today I became a citizen
    of the United States of America!"

SNOWPLOW MAN

for Rich

Hunched over his steering wheel,
He squints the road into focus.
His truck's headlights beckon him
Into the shimmering white curtain before him.
   The wipers
      sweep, sweep,
        left, right,
          brush, brush,
            back, forth,
              whisk, whisk away
The white wrapping on his windshield.

He concentrates on his confrontation with God's Alchemy,
The spinning swirl of water, cold air, low-pressure system
Moving up the coast, with its confetti of shiny petals
Fluttering to earth, insulating parched flowers with cold warmth.
The Driver stares and steers, gloved left hand on the wheel,
Right hand circling the Styrofoamed warmth of coffee.
His plow bares the road and scrapes its metallic song.
Round and round he goes, in repetition of his assigned task,
Pushing his endurance to undo the storm's relentless undoing
                        of what he has done.
He longs for warmth and rest, departure from the dark night
Which shimmers so brilliantly before him.

When God tires of twirling and agitating the elements,
The snow-show whispers its last white breath.
A dark curtain unfolds, replaces the storm's silvery screen.
Lifting his plow from the road, Snowplow Man turns for home.
His headlights sweep the blanketed landscape.
Somewhere in the night, where the light no longer carries,
Where its energy dissipates into darkness,

A cluster of pines stands as a glowing silhouette.
With their gathered snow, the evergreens
Are gowned in luminous silk; a huddle of tall brides,
Slightly bowed of white weight, as if paying homage
                                              to something.

PEMAQUID LIGHT

Every six seconds
the lighthouse spins its flash
above Muscongus Bay and John Bay
in its dutiful illumination of dawn.

Now, fog unfurls melancholy
like a steel-gray curtain,
blurs the dark sweep of Atlantic.
No sunrise. No morning prayers.

Disappointed, we turn from the fading night,
lean homeward, up the rocky bank, when
a shaft of pink flickers—a candle
puffing a mist of purple on the horizon.

The glowing sphere dilates
like an awakened eye, and in its slow rising,
floats as if it were a rose balloon in a violet sky.
Its blush unveils Monhegan Island.

Now the sun sparkles on water,
a path of glittering rubies
cast to our feet, an invitation.
There *are* morning prayers.

FISHING THE MADISON

Southwestern Montana

Beyond the crossing at *Three Dollar Bridge,*
the endless sweep of prairie sage
shimmers silver-green, like an ocean
flooding the foothills of the Madison Range,
lofty and jaggedly proud in the East.

The river's swish, gurgle and slap
pitches and tumbles in frothy crests,
slithers in rushing bubbles and whoosh,
riffles in bubbles and whoosh.

Now begins the upstream meditation.
Fly rod up, out, twelve o'clock, then three,
curled back, then flicked
into the long reach of an extended prayer,
casting upon the water
the *Wooly Bugger,* the *Elk-hair Caddis.*

Begins now the doubting, about
the missionary's uncertain gift,
how the offering looks from underneath,
the hook-hidden hope for communion
before the downstream reality, unanswered...

Begins now, the faith of repetition.

CRESTED BUTTE SUNRISE

for Hank Donovan

Hank and I shiver into our early morning run.
Our tentative steps brush harshly
through crystalline Colorado cold.
Downhill we shuffle, past Ponderosa Lodge,
then west on Gothic Road, squeaking
fresh footprints on the fluffy powder of snow.
Our exhaled breath puffs into an opaque mist
which hangs in the chilled air before us,
until we catch up to our own breathing,
run through it, disperse it.

Ptarmigans flutter ahead like winged snowballs.
Coyotes' yipping skips and trips over the horizon,
now a shimmering mirror of early morning light.
Our banter drifts and drops, as we are distracted
by the pale rose peaks of the Elk Mountains,
tall in the west, above the blushing snow.
We reach our turnaround point, circle each other
to retrace our steps home.
We halt, frozen in place.

Mt. Crested Butte towers above us,
jagged and black, framed and flamed
by the bleeding eastern sky, a heaven
dappled with purple and magenta bruises.
The rim of rising sun burns the mountain
with scarlet etchings, like trembling fingers
clutching the dark contour, lifting its rising fire
into the fading night sky.

I turn to my friend, his face burnt in the cold,
eyeglasses like two neon beacons in the glare.
He whispers, *something about Believing…*

We resume our run back to the Ponderosa,
    heads bowed, running softly,
    and we could not speak.

PRAYING AT 10,000 FEET

Wind River Mountains, Wyoming

Above Little Seneca Lake,
the eastward Ascension on Polecreek Trail
winds fourteen miles into the Bridger Wilderness.
Having climbed, we pitch tent, hoist the bear-bag.

In the surveillance of wild eyes, we bow
to the snow-capped Gods, Mount Gannet and
Mount Fremont, the Granite Spires reaching
like hands folded in high-altitude prayer.

At 10,000 feet, worship needs no voice.
It floats like a thought,
a litany of beatitudes
untethered in thin air...

Blessed are the wildflowers,
  Blue Lupine, the white of Columbine.
Blessed are the cougar, deer, and bear
  Which inhabit this wild peace.
Blessed be the cold purity of High-Country lakes,
  The mountains' jagged intrusion into heaven.
Blessed be the chorus of wind and snow,
  The white swirling of turbulent hallelujahs,
Blessed be the touchable stars, their
  Brilliant punctuation of night.
And Blessed be the trail, heavily stepped outward,
  Lightly stepped homeward, the homeward path.

Amen.

PERSONAL ACKNOWLEDGEMENTS

My wife Bonnie, who has reliably supported my commitment to poetry. She and my daughter Kristen saw the possibilities in my early writing. Without their encouragement, I would never have written my first poem.

Award-winning fiction writer Dennis Must became my early mentor. Patient and generous with his time, he taught me to find my voice and trust it.

Jeanette Maes, president of the Massachusetts State Poetry Association. Through her workshops she shared and inspired her students to fill the blank page.

Claire Keyes, extraordinary poet and Professor Emerita of English, Salem State University. Gifted teacher, she breathes life into the written word through her monthly Poetry Salon at the Marblehead Public Library.

Pennsylvania poet Christopher Bursk, my friend from the 2008 Juniper Writer's Conference. His imaginative writing inspires me to keep my pen in hand.

My fellow Tin Box Poets. Lee Freedman, Melissa Varnavas, Margaret Eckman, Paul Lahaie, Javy Awan, Estelle Epstein, Ray Whittier, Allen Marquis, Dave Somerset, Joan Clayman, all of whom have offered gentle criticism and new ways of looking at my own words; and Tim Sheehy, whose words reflect a special grace.

Marblehead Writers Group. Jean Callahan, Betsy Morris, Sandra Winter, Pic Harrison, Jack Butterworth, all of whom write vibrant and imaginative fiction, some of which finds a way into my poetry.

Yoon S. Byun, gifted photographer from Portland ME, for his permission to use the picture on the back cover.

Reverend Dennis Calhoun. Through his Tuesday morning Lectio Divina, he shares poems that illuminate the weekly gospel reading, thus validating that poetry can bring spiritual energy into our daily lives.

ABOUT THE AUTHOR

Clemens Carl Schoenebeck has had poems published in the *Aurorean, Caribbean Writer, Ibbetson Street Press, Midwest Poetry Review, Small Brushes*/Adept Press and other publications. Three of his poems have been nominated for The Pushcart Prize. He and his daughter Kristen were named featured poets of *Aurorean's* December issue in 2000.

His short stories have won various prizes in *Writer's World*, and Marblehead Festival of Arts.

In 2012, he won the poetry and fiction categories. His winning poem was selected for The Marcia Doehner Award, and his short story was awarded the first Georgette Beck Award.

His memoir, *Dancing with Fireflies,* is a story of his family living through the darkness and light of his mother's schizophrenia, and how poetry brought hope and healing.

Schoenebeck lives on the North Shore of Boston with his wife, Bonnie. His daughter's family lives nearby.

ABOUT THE COVER ARTIST

Angela Baldacci—one of the author's granddaughters—is the artist. Her painting was inspired by a photograph taken by her mother Kristen about twenty years ago. In the picture, the author walks with his granddaughters—Angela on his right, her sister Alexa on his left.

Through Angela's imagery, she illustrates the passage of time. Spring and summer are in the foreground as grandfather and granddaughters move through autumn toward the distant winter. Although that final season is closer for Schoenebeck than for his walking companions, they are together, sharing a portion of where the time went.

Baldacci is a recent graduate of Saint Michael's College, where she received her degree—magna cum laude—in media studies and digital arts.